Vijaya

AF665037

KAMALIKA MAJUMDER

BookLeaf
Publishing

India | USA | UK

Presentation by *BookLeaf Publishing*

Web: www.bookleafpub.com

E-mail: info@bookleafpub.com

ISBN: 9789360940386

First edition 2024

To those unknown and unsung female warriors of our struggle for Independence.

ACKNOWLEDGEMENT

First of all, I am and forever will be indebted to my teacher, Professor Rajasri Basu, who might not be with us in her corporeal presence on earth, but her indomitable spirit, her ideals and the effervescent zeal with which she envisioned a society in which women of marginalised group would one day find a space of their own, continue to ignite in my mind the urge to bring to fore the contributions of those self-effacing women who left their footprints on the murky roads of our historiography of freedom struggle, which got overshadowed by so many other giant footprints.

I'll be ever grateful to BookLeaf for appearing as a messiah to give my thoughts and ideas a proper shape and materialise the long-cherished dream of seeing them ensconced within two cosy covers. A big thanks to BookLeaf Publishing.

My colleague, Sri Samrat Moitra, who happens to be the grandson of great Bengali historian Sri Akshay Moitra, has always goaded me on to keep up writing on this subject and enriched me with his valuable suggestions.

Over and above everything, I owe a little munchkin the most, who, in spite of veritably deserving all my attention, bears me with all my distractions and frequent whims.

I

Vijaya

PREFACE

For so long we have only read about heroes who have laid their lives, and sacrificed their materialistic opportunities in life for the sake of liberating their beloved motherland. What we do not read or hear is the mention of hundreds of women belonging to the marginalised section of our society who also fought for the freedom of our country. So far pushed into oblivion, it is time that we look back to the valorous deeds of those valiant warrioresses and keep alive the flame of their patriotic spirits.

Jani Shikar

(circa 1203-1206)

Lo, behold, O mass of Rohtas,
The terrific trio here comes-
Kaili, Champai and Singai,
With the mighty enemies they vie.

It was a beautiful Sarhul night.
After a blissful merriment and fun,
The men to sleep's kingdom were gone.
Only a few were in sight.

At that time precise, just like a blight,
The enemy army sneaked in.
The Oraon Princess Singai with
Champai and Kaili stepped in
In men's attire.
Their men by the fire
Were still dozing.

The Oraon women gathered,
Enemy's advances they smothered
With bows, arrows and slings they battered
The enemy's pride.

(Jani Shikhar is a festival commemorating the famous battle where women from the Oraon aka

Kurukh tribe valiantly fought and protected their community from an invading army, defeating them in combat not once but twice.)

Abhaya

(Queen Abbakka Chowta: 1525-1570)

The Portuguese came first,
Captured Goa and moved southwards.
For the lust of power, to spread empire.

The ambitious fleet halted at Ullal—
The prosperous port ruled
By a young Queen called Abbakka.

The coastal Queen believed in equality,
Such that her army took in
Hindu, Muslim, Jain even Beary.

So when did Ãlvaro da Silveira invade,
The army held forth.
The army stood firm when came
João Peixoto and they braced up
To face admiral Marcarenhas too.

Three centuries before the Sepoy Mutiny,
A young Queen fought for her country.
Never did she yield, stood as a shield
To the last of her breath, she fought to death,
To save her subjects from slavery abject.

Yet how many remembers
  The first martyr Abbakka Chowta—
  The queen fearless,
  Rani Abhaya?

(Queen Abbakka Chowta is regarded as the first female freedom fighter (1525-1570). Abbakka not only thwarted the Portuguese army but also demonstrated her ability to unite people of diverse faiths against the Portuguese armed forces.)

Vijaya Dashami

(Kuyili, the Braveheart: 1700s-1780)

In the land of the brave-hearts on a blessed
morn,
In a tigress's womb, another tigress was born.
Raku the mother fought with a bull fiery and
fierce,
Saved her fields, cost her life, left the father in
tears.
Broken-heart, leaving his hearth, he moved into
Sivagangai,
Periyamuthan, the child's father became the
queen's spy.
Raised his daughter to be a warrior, made her
heart steely,
Swift as lightning, witty and stunning, that she
was—Kuyili.

Many times, evil designs the traitors and foes
devised,
Velu the Veera, the valiant queen exiled, was
saved
By Kuyili—the Commander in Chief who took
the vow
To free the beloved land from the British hand
anyhow.

On the blessed day of Vijayadashami, the tenth day,
The day of Victory, Kuyili resolved to have her sway.
She made her way, her army following by in disguise,
Each hiding weapons to take the British by surprise.
Storming into the arsenal smeared with oil all over,
Kuyili the first human bomb set herself on fire.
The Britons bent down, Velu reclaimed Sivagangai,
A tigress lay herself, nation's sake, Kuyili the Veeramangai.

(Kuyili was an army commander of Queen Velu Nachiyar who participated in campaigns against the East India Company in the 18th century. She was the first suicide bomber and the first woman martyr in Indian history.)

Rani Shiromani

(Rani Shiromani:1756-1812)

She vowed to protect her subjects,
The queen of Karnagarh,
The queen of the peasants
Pushed to marginality,
Refused to relinquish the rights
Of her poor subjects—
The rights of their own lands
To the rulers of the English Company.

The Chuars of the red lands were enraged.
Ready for a raging war
They braced themselves up
With courage, with fortitude and
A never-to-die attitude
Of a queen resolute, not to waver

Day by day, mustered forces they
And laid sieges on the white forts
Ran them out of provisions,
On the brinks of starvation,
The men of the Company bent,
Their weapons down they lay.

Then there was this mole,
Tipped off the strategy
Chalked out by queen not so easy,
Revealed to the captain of the Company,
Got the queen captured and sent to gaol.

Till death she held her stand, the first lady prisoner
Of the nation,
The enemies even revered her
for the steely determination.

(In the Midnapore district of West Bengal Rani Shiromani, queen of the Chuar or tribal farmers led the first revolt of tribal farmers against the British in 1798.)

Queen forever a Queen

(Rani Chennamma:1778-1829)

She was indefatigable,
Her every gesture, every elegant move
Bespoke royalty.
Head held high, chin up, not to give up,
She was the Queen of Kittur, she was Rani
Chennamma.

Righteousness was her religion.
So she raised arms against the
Draconian Doctrine of Lapse
And the battle was won.

Yet, she had a heart of gold.
Commissioner Chaplain pleaded
To release Stevenson and Elliot,
So did she, set them free from her hold.

But O naive Queen,
Trust the shifts of air,
The hot droughts, the nip of the cold,
Never trust the smooth smile fair
Or the glib words of a foe
Those are apt to feign.

Chaplain committed cease of war,
Not to interfere
In the princely state's affair.
As the Queen showed clemency,
Chaplain forgot the promise, the treaty.
Secretly seized the fort of Kittur,
Captured was the Queen,
Though she fought fiercely.

It was eras before the Sepoy Mutiny
That a regional Queen waged a war
To settle the wrongs of the Company,
She fought, she won, she lost—
Unwavered, she moved on—the pioneer.

(Also known as Kittur Rani Chennamma, the queen of Kittur, is hailed as one of the first female rulers to have rebelled against the British and is famous for the 1824 revolt against the East India Company who lost the first battle against her. This feat turned her into a folk hero in the Karnataka culture as well as the prime symbol of the independence movement.)

Jagrani

(Uda Devi Pasi: 1830-1857)

A hard battle it was;
A stiff strife,
On the shores of Gomti,
On the days of the Mutiny,
A dare-devil sniper
Shoots down a dozen number
Of white men.
And then...
The white men puzzled,
The white guns rattled,
Hither and thither,
Near and far,
And at last...
With a big blast
Roared Campbell's gun.
Down fell the rebel,
Faint sounded knell,
Gasping for breath,
Battling with death,
The mutineer lay.
'Finish him, fire!'
Off went the bullets dire.
Under the peepal tree
Quiet lay the soul free,

A zenana in man's attire.
Bombs and guns tucked under belt,
Some of them used, some left loaded,
A dozen whites she did slay
From the top of the tree.

Nearer came Campbell,
'A gutsy, adversary belle!'
Tipping his hat saluted he
The woman gritty—Uda Devi Pasi.
A Dalit woman, Maka Pasi's wife,
Used to protect Hazrat Mahal's life.
Courage and prowess made her
The women's wing commander.
At the battle of Sikanderbagh
Martyred was she
For the sake of her motherland,
To set the land free.

(Uda Devi is said to have been born in the village Ujriaon of Lucknow. She became an associate of Begum Hazrat Mahal, and formed a women's army, with herself as the commander. Her husband became a martyr in the battle at Chinhat. Uda decided to take revenge. When the British attacked Sikandar Bagh in Lucknow under Campbell, he was faced with an army of Dalit women. Uda Devi was one of them, who is said to have climbed over a 'pipal' tree and shot dead British soldiers. One soldier spotted someone in the tree and shot the person dead, and only then it was discovered that she was a woman.)

Avanti

(Avantibai Lodhi:1831-1858)

The Lodhi queen of Ramgarh,
The very name describes her—
Avanti! Go forward!
So was she, a stalwart.
A patriot in heart,
Dreamt that the world
Around her would be free
Of coercion, apathy and torture.
The imperialists she hated most,
Invoked others to join hands
To drive the whites away from the motherland.
Near Mandla at Khairi
She won the victory,
Claimed Mandla free.
But, with a vengeance, they returned,
The men of the Company, they learned
That there must be a traitor
Called the King of Rewa.
The queen fought with valour;
Yet, the traitor's troop
Scripted English win.
The undaunted queen
Her spirits not did droop,

Took up her sword fierce
Her bosom did she pierce.
Even before her breath
The queen quivered and said,
“God bless my country, my nation will live long,
One day she will be free, to sing freedom song.”

(Avantibai Lodhi was from the Lodhi tribe of India. She was a freedom fighter and the queen of Ramgarh. Avantibai used guerrilla tactics to fend off the British army. She took the blade from the guards’ sword and pierced it through herself, committing suicide on March 20, 1858, when she faced almost inevitable defeat in the war.)

The Heroines of Hool

(Santhal Revolt: 1855-1856)

They lived with love in their own land,
They hunted, tilled, were used to hard toil.
They were born to lead, to command-
The daughters and sons of the soil.

Yet the enemies came,
Their lands encroached upon,
Tried to quell, trample and tame
The original settlers with weapons.

The naive Santhal tribes fought back,
Sido, Kanho, Bhairav and Chand
Guts and courage did they not lack,
To hit hard at the brute imperial hand.

Murmu sisters—Sumi, Jhano and Phulo,
Resolved to avenge the wrongs the whites did.
Armed with machetes and spears, arrows and bows,
Ravaged the British camp, twenty soldiers they killed.

The fierce female martyrs, the Santhal sisters,
Even before the Great Sepoy Revolt,
Those heroines of Hool,
Those bravehearts,
Now un-remembered,
Gave the Brits the first jolt.

("Hool", the Santhal word for 'liberation movement' was led by Phulo and Jhano Murmu along with their brothers, Sido, Kanhu, Chand and Bhairav Murmu. Phulo Murmu and Jhano Murmu jumped into the battle fray with their brothers, and reportedly killed 21 British troops before they were martyred. The British brutally quelled the movement after killing over 25,000 tribal people. The Santhal Bidroho (revolt) of 1855-56 was in all probability, the fiercest liberation movement in India next to the "Sepoy mutiny" of 1857.)

Durga Dal

(1857 Sepoy Mutiny)

They sent their husbands to war.
They did not dither,
Nor did they shed tears,
As it was the Great War—
The Great Mutiny.
They believed it was their destiny
The glory to become martyrs' wives.
So, Mandar, Mundari Bai, Moti Bai
Called all—
'Churi farwai ke nevta,
Sindoor pochwai ke nevta.'
(A call to break our bangles
A call to wipe our vermilion)
Without the sacrifice of these women
There would have been no war martyrs,
History would have been otherwise written.

(Durga Dal was the women's regiment of the Queen of Jhansi. The women of Durga Dal did not fear widowhood; nor did they fear to fight on the battlefield itself. They fought and sacrificed their lives for the sake of the nation. Some of the women whose references have been found in sources are Mandari, Sundari Bai, Moti Bai and Mundari Bai.)

The Forgotten Warrioress

(Jhalkari Bai: 1830-1858)

On Plassy ground, a prophet pronounced,
A century later, a revolt will batter
This fiendish British Empire.
Days pass, pass years, and a century thus,
By the Ganges, the martial barrack ignites a
spark.
The glint hits the shore of Pahuj river
Bastion of Jhansi stands proudly here.
The fiery queen Lakshmi bears a flame in her
heart,
So does Jhalkari—a younker born in a Dalit hut.
Lakshmi's Captain, Jhalkari strides in lightning
speed,
Her sword sparkles, heart steely, full of grit.
White soldiers barged in to siege Jhansi's fort,
Ceaseless shelling to capture the queen to
Victorian court.
Comes forward Jhalkari disguising as the queen,
Stands by her Puran Kori, to save Jhansi from
ruin.
Straight goes the shell to kill the purported
queen,

Shields Puran his love, lets down own life in vain.
Hugh Rose the sly soldier grasps the tricks so fast,
Cons the lass saying that the queen has breathed her last.
Though despondent, the warrioress not let spirit go less,
Her scars bleed, bleeds her heart, fights she with jest.
At last, she drops, over her corpse the Brit horses hop,
Storms Jhansi's fort, stomps Jhansi's men, Mutiny's last hope.
A century and a decade less, the nation breaks free of shackles,
Dear nation, do you remember her, the mighty Dalit warrioress?

(Set against the historical background of India's first freedom struggle against the British, this poem is about Jhalkari Bai, a forgotten name in the history of India's freedom struggle. Born in 1830 to a Dalit farmer family in a small village near Jhansi (now in Uttar Pradesh, India), Jhalkari Bai showed sparks of extraordinary bravery and guts since childhood. She learned archery, horse riding and was adept in all kinds of feats that a seasoned soldier possesses. In her youth, she was inducted into Durga Bahini, the Women's Battalion in the army of Lakshmi Bai, the Queen of Jhansi, the mighty queen of Jhansi as well as one of the most prominent figures of the Sepoy Mutiny of 1857. The Sepoy Mutiny was the first revolt by the Indians against the British empire which set forth its reign in India in the year 1757 with their triumph at the Battle of Plassey. Jhalkari Bai was a crucial figure in the Sepoy Mutiny because by dint of her excellence as a soldier and for her subtle wit, she rose to the position of the chief advisor of Queen Lakshmi. Besides, Jhalkari had a striking resemblance to the physical appearance of Queen Lakshmi Bai. In 1858, when the British army besieged Jhansi fort, Jhalkari disguised herself as the queen and faced Hugh Rose, the Commander of the British force. Jhalkari put up a valiant fight but by a con trick of General Rose, she was misinformed that the Queen of Jhansi had been killed. This and the death of her husband Puran Kori before her own eye demoralized Jhalkari and on April 5, 1858, the daring Dalit warrioress accepted martyrdom.)

A Ray of Hope

(Asha Devi Gurjari: Year of Birth Unknown -1857)

Asha was her name,
A daring warring dame.
No wrongs did she bear,
For her country did she care.
Felt the need to gather
Women from near and far.
Taught them to fight,
Set the wrongs right.
'Twas the first battle of Independence,
Igniting was Asha Devi's utterance—
"Against injustice of all kinds,
Women, do not keep quiet!
You shouldn't lag behind."
Went forward all female army,
Led by Asha Devi Gurjari.
Face to face they fought,
Huge loss to the English they brought.
She fought valiantly with all her might,
As the evening set, the red horizon in sight,
A bullet pierced through her slender body
She lay on the ground, a hope did she carry-
In her heart; quiet and still she lay, dreaming
Her nation will be free someday.

Beloved motherland will be free someday.

(Asha Devi Gurjari is portrayed as a leader to a large number of young girls and women and it is stated that on May 8, 1857, she along with a large number of other women attacked the British army and died while fighting.)

Veerangana

(Mahaviri Devi:
Unknown -1857)

It was said that
Being a Bahujan, being a woman
Was a blight—
She defied it.
The lower caste women
And children were made to do
Tasks lower even.
Mahaviri Devi, a Bahujan,
Raised her voice, opposed.
'Dignity for all', claimed she.
A woman of substance,
Desired to see the nation free
And its women.

The great Mutiny beckoned her.
Mahaviri formed a female front.
Off went a formidable fight,
Many British soldiers subdued
But at last...
Mahaviri breathed last
Kissed her dear earth-beloved motherland.

(In 1857, Mahaviri Devi made a group of 22 women and attacked the British. She fought bravely and killed many British. Finally, she herself was killed by them and along with her 22 other unknown women died.)

Women of Ulgulan

(Munda
Ulgulan:1895-1900)

To suppress the uprise
The Commissioner reached Ranchi.
He with his entourage knocked on
Gaya Munda's door.
Unanswered, he rapped, kicked, thumped
On the yard floor.
A constable in a bid
to force open the door,
hit, hit and hit.
Soon he came out,
Tattered and battered.
The commissioner gave out a shout—
'Come out, come out!
Or else fire will burn your house.'
Still quiet.
Resolute, the commissioner threw
Matchstick on the thatched roof,
And the fire brew.

Out came Gaya Munda
Out came his wife Maki
And daughters—
Lembu, Thegi, Nagi.

Each holding weapons,
Sticks, swords and bows.
Maki beat hard the commissioner,
With an axe once she killed an officer.
Carrying children on the left
These women did wield
The weapons on the right.
They were women of Ulgulan.
For Birsa, they sounded the call of Clarion.

(Women had a strong role in Munda Ulgulan, in 1895-1900, against the British Raj. Women like Gaya Munda, Maki Munda, Lembu, Thegi and Nagi fought and at the same time gave their lives to protect the motherland. It is worrisome that women who have taken an equal share in the making, creation and struggle of society have not got due respect in history.)

The Tana Women

(Tana Bhagat Movement:1914)

The Tana Women
They opposed the injustice,
The wrongly placed taxes
Imposed upon them,
They were Tana Bhagats.
They opposed exploitations
Of all kinds—
Imperial or feudal.
They were Tana Bhagats.
They were believers of non-violence,
They had Litho Oraon and
They had Devmani Oraon,
Who believed in the Nature credence,
Carried with them the creed of a free race.

(Tana Bhagat movement was started to stop the evil practices, which were taking place in the Oraon community of Chotanagpur and to oppose the Jamindars policies, which were exploiting the Oraon people directly.)

Into the Oblivion

(Bina Das:1911-1986)

You remember her?
Who nestled a skyful
Of love for you, dear?
Loved you more
Than she loved herself.
Nor for that matter,
Did she ever care
For a thing, a feeling
Called self-love.

Many of her peers
Chose a life of
Security—marriage or job.
She had chosen you.
She held the tinder
Within her hands,
For the love of you.

You remember her?

On that day fateful
Inside the Senate Hall,
Dared she fling
The glance glaring
And a fire-ball
Full of wrath and gall
To Stanley Jackson
The then Governor of Bengal .

Do you remember her,
O dear, dear Nation?
She sacrificed her all
To bust the imperial bastion.
To rid you of your fetters
She embraced incarceration.

Do you remember her,
O dear, dear Freedom?
Did you even recognize her
When at roadside she lay infirm?
An octogenarian,
Devoid of all means
She left your earthly kingdom
Sans any caring bliss.

Bina Das was her name,
Never she hankered after
Flashy, flitting fame
Nor ever a glutton for silver.

All that she desired was to
Adorn you with wings of
Freedom, to shade you
With a wide liberal sky.

Do you know why?
Because she loved you
More than she loved herself.
O dear, dear Free Nation
Do you remember her?
Do you even care?

(Bina Das was an Indian revolutionary and nationalist from West Bengal. She was born to social workers and educationist parents, who were deeply involved in the Brahmo Samaj and the freedom struggle.
Das was a member of Chhatri Sangha, a semi-revolutionary organisation for women in Kolkata. On 6 February 1932, she attempted to assassinate the Bengal Governor Stanley Jackson, in the Convocation Hall of the University of Calcutta. The revolver was supplied by another freedom fighter Kamala Das Gupta. She fired five shots but failed and was sentenced to nine years of rigorous imprisonment.)

Old Lady Gandhi

(Matangini Hazra: 1870-1942)

A short frail woman
Old and wizened,
Yet striding along,
Leading her gang
To Tamluk police post,
To capture and ensure
The administration
Of Tamluk in people's power.

Matangini the old lady
Stout, stern and steady
Was Gandhi's worshipper.

The all-female gang
Vande Mataram they sang,
And proceeded to snatch
Freedom for their motherland.

'Boom, boom, bang!'
The police gun rang,
Matangini fell,
On the ground, she fell,
Yet the flag in hand,
The Iron Lady made command—

'Go forward! Win freedom!'

(Matangini Hazra was an Indian revolutionary who participated in the Indian independence movement until she was shot dead by the British Indian police in front of the Tamluk Police Station on 29 September 1942. She was affectionately known as Gandhi Buri, Bengali for old lady Gandhi.)

Savitri

(Helen

Lepcha:1902-1980)

A simple upland lass,
Her innocence breathed
Purity of the Himalayan hills
She belonged to.
As she grew, she saw
Her nation fettered
With imperial chains.
Silently she suffered
To see her people in pain,
Slighted, ignored and pushed
Away to invisibility.
In the western part of the country,
A simple frail man was up against
The British.
He called upon his countrymen
Foreign goods to abandon.
To be self-reliant, to weave
Yarns on the spinning wheels
And make our own things.
The young upland girl
Worshipped the old man,
She joined the Charkha Andolan.

People of Bihar were flooded under;
The young girl reached there
To provide succour.
Her devotion earned Gandhi's admiration,
She was called on
At Sabarmati Ashram.
Helen Lepcha—hailing from the hills
Was named Savitri—the woman with zeal.
Led the hill people in the Movement
Non-Cooperation,
Relentless to shake the base of the British
bastion.

With a heart full of sympathy and care
She felt the need to unite the labourers and the
farmers—
The most deprived those are.
All along her life, she took the pledge
To help those denied of all privileges.
All praise to the simple highland lass, Salute!
The free people of the free nation should follow
her suit.

(Helen Lepcha of the Lepcha tribe, was an ardent follower of Mahatma Gandhi. Her influence over her people made the British restless. She was shot at, imprisoned and hounded but she never lost courage.)

Rani

(Gaidinliu:1915-1993)

A young belle nimble
Was darting through
The hilly jungle
As the dark grew.

Hanged her brother—
The rebel sought after,
The police thereafter
Hounded her.

The gutsy sister
Took upon her
The baton of the brother
Hereafter.

Spread the word everywhere
'Stop paying tax to white officers,
They unleash torture
And destroy our culture.'

The police enraged

Assam Rifles engaged
To nab her
From wheresoever.

Hills after hills she wandered
Propelled by the fervour
And memory of her brother
Unwavered, she spread her word.

She was Gaidinliu,
Named by Nehru
As Rani Gaidinliu.
Caught and jailed
For life, the court held,
The people's leader.
The Independence after
The court order
At last released her.
As long as she lived,
For the people she lived—
Kabui—the ancient, hilly tribe.

(Gaidinliu was born on January 26, 1915, in the present-day Tamenglong district of Manipur and died in 1993. The Naga spiritual and political leader, who led an armed uprising against the British in Manipur, Nagaland and Assam, belonged to the Rongmei tribe which is also known as Kabui.)

The Beloved Mother

(Puttalimaya

Devi Poddar: 1920-1984)

She heard of the battle,
The struggle that the
Country was grappling with
The struggle for freedom.
At a remote corner
In a hilly hamlet
She bore a dream
In her tender heart.
She dreamt one day
The nation will call her
To join hands with the strugglers.

At last, came the day,
The Father of Nation
Blew the clarion
To claim Swaraj.
'Let the hills pay
Their due to our
Beloved motherland,

Let’s form a band
To protect the country.’
Thus said Putalimaya—
The 'beloved mother'
Of the Gorkha clan.

A disciple of Bapu
Went she through
Long duress of
Imprisonment.
Felt empathy for
The poor, the downtrodden,
The children of the same God...
Yet,
The hatred, the resentment
They were meted out to.

The nation got freedom;
But did not become free
From inequality—
Of wealth, honour
And opportunity.
Putalimaya strove along—
Relentless, she went strong
Against all odds,
To stand by the people
Who belong
To the roots.
People of the hills thus,

Fondly remember their
Mataji in days' prayer.

(Puttalimaya Devi Poddar, a Gorkha lady and a heroine of the nationalist movement of India challenged not only the imperial order but also the social order of the day.)

Women of Warli

(Warli

Revolt: 1945)

For their own land
They had to pay,
To the lusty landlord
They had to give away
More than half
The crop they yielded of.

They fed the feudal lords,
With their own crops,
Themselves they starved.
Served as bonded labour,
Their caste didn't favour,
Social calling that history carved.

The women of Warli resisted,
For them existed
Dishonour, torture and disfavour.
They sent their men to war,
Against exploitation of all kinds—
Feudal or imperial—
The two hands in gloves.

The men went underground,

The women stayed home
To protect the child and the old,
To take care.
The bayonet lashed at them manifold,
Yet they did not care,
Nor did they fear.

These women, these little ancient
Women of caste, colour and tribe,
Were part of the revolt,
They stood in the front
As a shield to appear,
For their men to steer
The movement of Warli—a jolt
To the imperial ruler, to the feudal master.

(The involvement of the tribal women in the Warli revolt was supported by the Kisan Sabha leader, Godaveri Parulekar, also known lovingly as Godutai (elder sister) by the adivasis. Women followed Godutai. Women would speak at meetings about the oppression they faced and would encourage other women to join the struggle.)

Appiko

(

Appiko Movement:1983)

The women made a resolution.
Resolved to stave off the demons
To save their gods.
Pristine gods they were
Resilient and stout,
Heads held high up,
Blissful hands stretched out.
Their feet fixed firm into the ground
To save the earth from crumbling down.
They hailed the fecund rains
Breathing life into earth's veins;
And thus, they kept the clime salubrious.

Then came the fiends, the Archfiends
With shears, saws, axes and hatchets
To knock, to chop, to hack, to fell the gods.
Behold! Come rushing the womenfolk
'Stop the logging!' They invoke.
The lumbermen recede not, at daggers drawn,
The ladies clasp their gods—the trees
'Strike us first!' They utter in unison.
Overnight they guard the trees
Embracing with all their might

Till the loggers retreat, move out of sight.
Thus sylvan soil was saved from an imminent
Chaos
With the earth's élan restored, a triumph of
Peace it was.

(This poem is a tribute to the female grassroots-level activists participating in the Appiko Movement (1983). The movement was waged as a protest to the rapid deforestation due to the unplanned and rampant urbanisation programme that was being carried out in Uttar Kannada, of Karnataka state of India. In September 1983, a group of women whose sustenance depended on the forest regions of Uttar Kannada, got united and planned to launch a protest by hugging (Appiko means hugging in Kannada language) the trees. Panduranga Hegde, a social activist conceived the idea following the Chipko movement in Uttarakhand, a decade ago. With their firm resolution, the women moulded the Karnataka government to accede to their wishes and thus they saved the region from soil erosion, permanent denudation of forestry and destruction of essential spice plants and herbs.)

II

The New Birth

Foreword

Among the myriad miraculous workings of God, the most wonderful, wonderous and unique is perhaps the creation of a human baby—how a life is ensconced, nurtured and developed into a miniature human being within the safe abode of the mother's womb. A life within a life. Throughout this amazing journey of nine or ten months, not only a new baby is born but the baby itself transforms its mentor into an altogether new identity also. When a woman becomes a mother, she experiences a metamorphosis of sorts. A new life. Life of a mother. A new phase in her life. So the process of giving birth happens both ways. With the birth of the child, a mother is born also. The child gives birth to the mother. In this compilation, the process of childbearing right from fertilization to the birth of the child is encapsulated within forty-two crisp haiku poems. Vives tu vida!

Sowing

Seed sown in ground,

The soft ground, the caring,

Ensconces it deep inside.

Nourishing

The seed gets nourished,

The sustenance for its life,

The *juissance* scarlet.

Growing

Slowly, sprouts a life,

Inside the dark puzzling cave,

The mystery unknown.

Beats

A sesame seed look,

As five weeks go, flicker starts

Of the tiny heart.

Senses

Size of a lentil,

To hear, to smell, to taste

Life is equipped with.

Limbs

Seven weeks pass on,

Limbs grow, all paddles and tail,

Echoes of a common past.

First Move

Fluttering of limbs,

Though not palpable, begin

Primal neural path.

Grape

Grape-size tiny life

Full anatomy in spread

Disappear the tail.

They Nail

The skin translucent

The tiny kumquat bends limbs,

Tiny fingers nail.

Care the Fig

Almost fully formed,

Kicking, stretching, hiccupping

The size of a fig.

Reflexive

Fiddling with fingers

Twirling the toes, spouting mouth,

Lime-sized little thing.

Fingerprint

Faint fingerprints,

Veins visible through skin,

Thirteen weeks pea pod.

Impulses

Facial muscles twitch,

Impulses stir tiny brain,

Tiny mouth, thumb sucked.

Apple of Eyeball

Eyelids are shut tight,

Eyeballs senses rays of light

Apple-sized small thing.

Upright

Head growing upright,

With patterning of the scalp

Positioning tiny ears.

Stronger the Bond

Umbilical bond,

Blood is thicker than water,

Stronger grows the cord.

Fluttering

Flexing arms and legs

Little movements palpable,

Stimuli forming.

Voices Heard

Step on nineteen weeks,

Womb receives the mother's voice

Five senses, one cord.

I Share My Morsel

Sharing the same food,

Swallowing the grub slowly,

Through the pathway of food.

Step-up

Movements go rapid,

From flutter to full-on kicks,

On the wall of the womb.

Miniature

Growing on and on,

Lips and eyebrows more distinct,

A miniature.

Echoes from the Cave

Harking to all sounds,

The little thing responses,

Reminisce later.

Change is Life

Waiting for a change,

Chubbier days coming ahead,

Pretty ear of corn.

Smoothening

Wrinkled skin gets smoothened,

Tiny hair covering head,

Swimming through the cave.

Life Breathing Life

Pulsating movements,

Inhaling, exhaling fluid

Life breathes into life.

A mind not Mine

Waking and sleeping

With a brain active and fast,

A mind though not formed.

Wink of an Eye

I blink, I wink at

Some light from outside the cave,

With fine eyelashes.

Wee Wits

Sinews getting strong

To function outside the cave,

Wit nestled within the crown.

A Room of Its Own

Day by day grow on,

You need space, room of your own,

More spacious than a cave.

Head Turner

Growing buxom more,

Turning head this side and that,

Kingdom of the cave.

Stronger the Limbs

The cave more spacious,

Bond stronger with cave-owner,

Seven weeks to go.

Narrow is the Path

Crown not hard enough,

Path to glory is narrow,

Squeeze through a narrow path.

Impulses

Axons joining hands,

Impulses developing,

Breathing health inside.

Snug

Moving to and fro,

Getting snug inside the cave,

Honeydew melon.

Casting Off

Losing lanugo,

Body wax getting thinner,

Protected in cave.

Sweet Pie

A bunch of sweet chard,

Sweetness growing intense more,

Smiles the sweetie pie.

Getting Ready

Fingernails all formed,

Ready for the big event,

Anytime may come.

Almost There

The dark cave gets sealed,

The munchkin grows big baby,

Growing and growing.

That Blessed Moment

Through the opening

Of nestling cave emerges

The fair cherubim.

The First Cry

Excruciating

Pain she bears for the first cry

all that she craved for.

The First Touch

All her existence

Feels eternal joy when she

Holds the weeny one.

A New Birth

The birth of a child

Gives birth to another life—

Birth of a Mother.

III

Colours of Life

Proem

Life has many shades of colours to offer. It's joyful, sad, enchanting, thrilling and yet mysterious, and enigmatic. This compilation of eight long poems tries to colour the reader's mind with strokes of those different shades taken from life's palette.

For the Love of the Sea

The Sea beckons me.

Yearning for my fingers

To lull his crest,

While my lips kiss

His feet with jest

To fathom his love for me.

The Sea promises me of Eternity.

He holds my hand, we touch the horizon

And riding on his stallion,

We set for the Eternal Unknown.

Nature begot me.

I'm the Immanence. I'm the Earth.

I'm the Cimmerian enigma—

In my womb, Man took his first birth.

The Sea waits for me.

With shells he bedecks

The seaboard blanche.

Souvenir par amour.

On a night wrapped up in

An ethereal moonshine

The solitary silver shore lies supine.

The flamboyant shells I garner

One after another.

With the touch of my finger

They open their pout ajar.

Speckled shells—nestling inside

A drop of tear or a simper,

A joy exotic or a woe sombre.

Nothing do I hold,

I fold the petals of the shells

And I plant them on the waves' fold.

The wave whisks away with his largess,

To root them at the nadir—

Ensconced in obscurity, swathed in a daze.

The Brine is a conjurer, a conjurer is he.

He juggles with a tear or a smile dear,

And swaps them in a jiffy.

Back when I will be,

The Sea will wait for me,

Adorning the span of sand with shells

Carrying in their womb

The morphed tears—the pearls—

Souvenir par amour...

For me, the love of the sea—

L’amour de la mer.

Road to Summit

The black night was bleary and bleak.
Sleep failed those two men inside the South
Cole camp—
Nerves taut, both sitting awake.
Counting hours, biding their time,
Earnestly praying to the Almighty
To offer a favourable clime
For the morn to come and for the day.
•••
Time ticks off...
Crimson streaks adorn the horizon far off.
The men brace themselves up
With essential gears—
The ice-axe, the crampon, the harness, the rope
Among the mighty tools myriad others.
The duo eyed each other, exchanged words
unspoken.
They set out for the conquest, determined and
spirits unshaken.
•••
Whacks and hacks of the axe cleaving through
the frozen ice stiff
Two brave hearts scaling the steep heights of the
impervious massif.

Daunting the challenges of the goliath, the monolith called the Everest,
Enigmatic, abstruse, towering over the Earth, the Himalayan crest.
Hillary and Tenzing went trudging along, all hardships did they embrace
To script Man's victory, setting foot on the world's apex.
Not a mere conquest it was, ‘twas a heraldry, a celebration
Of Man's ardour, resilience, legerity, and gritty determination.
The Spartan spirit, the Promethean prowess of the maiden achievers
Remain as inspiration as long as the montage of life Man traverses.

Motherland

'Where are you from? This side of the border or
that side? Tell.'
'What's in the name of the land? Nature is just
the same dear, without any fail.
Nature knows not any racial divide, nor
any barb-wire fence she abides by.
Could any frontier change the blue of the sky
ever?
Both lands, the same vast firmament spans over.
Could ever any border Force snatch the verdure
of the vale
That spreads alike on either side of the line?
Neither could a strike of a pen ever change the
melody
Of the Robbin that sings through the pristine
woods of pine.
Ask the river that has flowed since times
unknown, she knows—
That the divided lands only take new names,
On both sides of the fence
Every workday of an everyman remains the
same.
No Berlin Wall ever could divide the hearts that
did long
Across the barrier, to see each other;

So, my dear friend, do not you bother
To which soil I belong.
I'm the daughter of Mother Earth,
From her fecund womb did I take birth.
I'm grounded to my roots and that I'm proud of.
A passion paces through my veins to protect and preserve
The oneness of the human race that will be erased with time
The dividing marks of Borders on the Atlas—
Ringing in a new era for humankind, the holy bell will chime.'

Ikigai

The vermillion streaks in the eastern sky, the
rubicund orb glowing
Tiny globular dew drops resting softly on the
green grass unknowing.
The resonant river goes warbling by the verdant
woodland sheen
Making the coppice redolent, blooms the night
flowering jasmine.
Snowy mountain-crown glorious with the
maiden sunshine
Ceaselessly flow the countless untiring waves of
the brine.
The star-spangled canopy vast, arched over the
homey earth
The array of blithe glowworms gleaming with
mirth.
The septuple shades of the Sol god's steadfast
stallions
Stretched across the infinite Empyrean
Fills my heart with ecstasy, with a humble
wonder
What a stellar artist, a supreme wizard is the
Creator!
The mighty charms of all of His beauteous
worldly creations

Are my reasons to live, my ikigai—the bountiful source of inspiration.

The Princess Precious

In the Delphic darkness of my sylvan womb,
Like an Amaranthine bud did she bloom.
Nine months and nine days did I nurture
My dream to welcome that moment of rapture
When the floret burst out into full blossom
I caressed, ensconced it into my warm bosom.
Then I set sails on the vast sea—the Main called life.
Clasping my Amaranth tight—tides of hope in rife.

Out of the blue, the storm lashed, nature's fury unleashed,
My little canoe baffled, tumbling and fumbling in the blitz.
Heart and soul I prayed, to the Saviour for succour,
With the touch of the divine wand, brought the miracle
The Greatest Disposer, the Greatest Conjurer.
Thus emerged from the tender floret, the lovely little lass
Crowned with a golden tiara, silver sceptre in hand—the princess.

Her eyes spoke of assurance fearless, eyes deep and glib—
"Fear not dear mother, together we'll ride the wave
And bridle the forces evil, together we'll harness earth's zing
And a rainbow-clad sky I promise you of, a dewy dawn will I bring."
Joie de la vie—my princess—she fills my heart with blissful gaiety,
God's gift she's to me, she is the spring of all my felicity.

The Golden Shower

Golden Shower, O fair Golden Shower,
Will you let the austral breeze kiss
The tender pout of your amber flower?
A pensive soul in the desolate lee,
For whom your flowers bloom—tell me?
Those truant clouds, a heart tear-stained,
Did you hear the wind's whisper when it rained?
Golden Shower, O dear Golden Shower,
Was it a folly of your fickle fatuity
To offer the floret, its guileless beauty?
The Oriole painted your petals
With its fiery quills,
The flutters in your heart's vessel, the ripples.
Golden Shower, O darling Golden Shower,
The Nor'westers will carry my billet-doux for
you,
No more tryst, mon chéri, adieu, adieu!

The Offering

Thou my heart's blood, my pilot, my guiding spirit—
Shipwrecked, I was astray on the forlorn sea.
The chopping waves, the stygian deep, the nebulous night,
I sought refuge in the solace of thy feet.
In love and lovelessness, I pined for thee, in impersonal desire;
Thou filled my heart with boundless ecstasy, the nectar of thy love—the ambrosia.
The fevered heart, the wary mind, the desolate soul parched—
Thy blissful numbers replenish, assure me of the treasure I searched.
Thy words are benediction, O my King of Kings, thou Unmoved Mover,
I cleave through the endless sea with thou, my helmsman, the numinous Maker.

The Other Traveller

It was the month of November.
A misty evening shrouding itself
In a grey cloak, lookin' sombre.
I was on my way home
From an errand.
The bare woods hushed,
The stinging north wind errant.
Combing my way through
The Maple's mum and
The blanched Birches,
A strange stillness grew
In the heart of darkness.
The prescient call of the wise bird
Piercing through the dumb wall
Of a gelid earth.

A tap on my nape—
Startled, I looked back.
None.
Only the dark hollow,
Only the stubborn blank.
I paced up and fast as I sped,
I saw someone, spang ahead.
"Who goes there? Wait."
Stifling silence of a moment;

Then came the reply
In a voice frigid and dry.
"A traveller, a wayfarer."
"Which way you go fella, whither?"
"A long way hence- far, far, afar."

Moved fast the traveller
And fast followed I
Yet I couldn't be at par
Stayed lagging behind.
Then,
Under an old oak, beside an old brook
Stopped my companion,
Raised one hand as if to beckon.
Under that pristine oak tree reached I,
Through the primal night spoke my ally—
"Beyond this wild, old lave lies my land,
Thither I go now, farewell my friend."
"No canoe here to ferry you over my dear,
You can't leave before the dawn, I fear."
"My vessel has left the port long ago,
I came here alone, alone will I go."
"Who are ye, mate? What name? Say.
Let's know each other, look here, I pray."

The dark stillness spawned on end,
Slowly, oh so silently turned my friend.
A vague shadow-unearthly, undefined, obscure,

Two blazing eyes, gazing, yet un-human for sure.
Could I not stand that trenchant gaze
I took my eyes off, gripped in a daze.
Time ticked off, I looked back again,
I found none—
Merged my friend was, into the haze.

Lookin' for my pal I stretched my sight-
Towards the horizon, dimmed by the night.
Then...all of a sudden,
From deep down the night's cavern,
A soft voice crooned along—
“In between the coming and going,
A defined path we all traverse;
Be it smooth or be it harsh
We walk strong my mate,
We walk strong.
Until the path ends.
By the old river Lethe
The path ends.
Down the stream, we sail along,
The vessel goes
To the other shore,
To the vale of the Shadows."

Memories

Standing on the silvery
Shore of memory
Like a squirrel I
Keep garnering
Grains of words
And glances and
Smiles and frowns.
Away from the shore,
In the inland of life,
I keep nibbling
The taste, the flavours
Of those tiny savoury grains.

Love-doves

By the seaside
On some high rocks
They scrambled up.
The towering serpents
Of the sea trying to
Lash out at the rocks
To spit venoms
Got contained by the
Shields of rocks.

By the seaside
On some high rocks
They scrambled up
To save their love
From the serpents below
On the crowded, dingy
And sordid dungeon
Spitting venoms that
Killed humanity.
But...
Nature hid two doves
To save their love.

Orange City

An orange coloured sun
Hovering on the wine coloured
Sky over the cerulean blue sea
Paints the town orange.
The promenade rimmed with
An array of tamarisk trees
Catching the hue
Paints the town orange.
The gentle petite houses
With lilac coloured walls

Paints the white town orange!

The Nectar

They came walking hand in hand,
Through the paved promenade,
They slowly stepped
Down the shell-dotted rocks
Onto the vast sway of the Bay.
To the call of the sea
They answered promptly.
Gingerly they walked step in step,
Into the wavy tapestry.
They played gleefully
Like butterflies, like two goldfish
Wiggling and giggling to relish
Each drop of the nectar called love.

Casuarina

The sage green casuarina
Standing serene along
The silvery beach.
Yonder the cyan-blue sea
Raising its celadon hood
With foamy mouth
About to lash out on the shore.
The casuarina catches the zephyr

And contains the advancing serpent
Raising its hood
Making breakers and surfs
Mingling with the
Scintilla of soulful
Vibes oozing across the brine.

The Pixie

She was on a spree,
A free soul, a free mind
Fluttering, flapping and flitting
Like the tiny creatures
With colourful wings.
All around the city she whisked
And scooted and pranced
On her own sweet will
Just the frisky winged creature
Taking its hues from the rainbow,
The little pixie bellbird.

The Orbit

For her, he meant the world.
She severed all ties with
The world outside
As he was the world to her.
He was her sun.
She revolved around him.

She renounced all her feats
To bathe in his reflected light.
But after years of having
A constant planet,
The sun in him
Regarded it like a satellite mere.
He disdained the pale
Worn-out satellite dim,
Refused to share his shining beam,
Sans the light, sans the warmth
Of her sun, she withered.
The distance widened between
The sun and its planet,
And one day she decided to
Change her orbit.

Treasure-trove

Everyone adores him,
Admires him,
He is worshipped by many.
He is a star
In the tinsel town.
Fans see him winning hearts
Either in a big hall
Or in the cosy corner
Of their small houses.
He talks, he glances,

He dances, he even sings
To the lilting tunes
To reign in their hearts.
He rules.
But they never saw him
In the recluse of his
Own house.
In the palatial mansion
He has a small nook.
Nobody is allowed there.
The superstar keeps
His treasure-trove there.
A basket full of marbles,
Ping-pings, a cricket ball,

Some colour pencils and
A notebook full of scribbles.

Strength

One day I was
Taking a stroll
Through furrowed meadow
On a winter afternoon
By the riverside.
As I settled myself
On a cosy bench
In a discrete corner

Under an old oak
A boy came paddling
His shabby Hercules.
He sat on the cold grass
Took out his pencils
And started sketching
The sky and the river.
I asked him,
"What's your name, boy?
You live nearby?"
Engrossed in his drawing,
He mumbled,
"I'm Fahad, Fahad means Lion."
Amused, I said,
"So you must be very powerful, no?"
"Fahad is my name. I've no one.

Like a lion, I can win over
My weakness and one day
I'll be victorious."
"Good luck to ye," Said I.
"But, what is your strength, say?"
"My art," said Fahad.
Just then...
Against the background of the pale
Evening sky I could see the setting
Sun red and Fahad holding
His hands up as if praying.

"Where's the drawing, Fahad?"
I was puzzled.
"Look at the sky again."
Surprised, I saw two suns in the sky!

Pestilence

The ancient tree
With its wise head
Held upwards
And stretching hands
Wide, thinks of the first
Rain it witnessed.
The refreshing feel,
The first cooling drops
Enthralled the tree-
Then but a seedling.
Ages after, the tree
Felt the same rejuvenation,
That cooling drops,
In a time when the
World is grappling with pestilence!

Question

Brick by brick a building builds,
Drop by drop an ocean,
Grains of sand form a land,

How many tears bleed an emotion?
Emotion exudes love or
Love oozes passion?
What is passion
Without emotion?

An Autumn Evening

As the autumn
Slowly wraps the
Foggy shawl around itself,
And decks its tiara
With beads of dewy pearls,
The wide land fallow
Takes a pinch of vermillion
From the blue casket of the sky
And puts it on its broad forehead.
Conch shells blow, lamps lit up
At the tulsi shrines at villagers' huts,
Evening dews gather on the grass blades,
Winter is about to descend on earth.

Wrath

Over the turquoise stream,
The sturdy bridge
Makes a perfect bend.
The rigid steels forming

The contour and the bars
Holding the structure firm
Have never seen the river
So fierce, so fuming with anger.
The arched support looked on
And kept pondering and wondering
How, all of a sudden, with sheer wrath
The river swept away the hills and hillocks
With gargantuan waves towering over.

The Glass

Waiting for many years
Of shrivelled winter leaves,
At last, he came yesterday
When I and you were
Collecting clouds
Sauntering through the shady terrace.
His glassy fingers touched my temple
And startled, “I knew you would be here!”,

On some moon-soaked eve,
The nimbus clouds blurred
The eyes of the naive nymph,
She lost her heart to a man’s prince.
Crystalline heart, the prince mistook
It to be crystal ball to toy with.

Alas! In an unmindful moment,
He broke the fragile ball!

For eons, you and I, we
Did not count waves in ocean,
It is, said that the salt of the
Nymph’s tears mingled with
The salty seas.

At last, yesterday he came.
On the soggy sand of the
Ochre shore he scratched
And said, “Look! I’ve written your name!”
Forgetting fiddling with the clouds,
I turned towards the shore.
The receding ripples were
Cautiously holding the sandy name
Within the glassy fingers.
I saw a glassy face smiling at me,
“I knew you would be here!”

Debt

This is the season of ennui,
How long will this tenuous light survive?
So long as it remains to pay its debt
To this mortal earth.
The debt is beyond repayment though.

The stubbled meadow holds an
Inexhaustible void.
The pale twilight silently
Embraces the solitary darkness.
The coy, sombre land
Draws the foggy veil on its sombre face.

On its barren bosom the heath
Holds a tapestry of heather—
That's all the glory it holds,
That's all it can pay to its
Debt to the munificent earth!

Girlie Days

Once we were girls.
We had a school
With stubborn walls that
Seemed to us
As tall as Mt. Everest.
Thick, rotund pillars
To play hide-and-seek
Behind them.
Jacaranda noons to
Colour the canvas of

Our wishy-washy minds
With dreams of one
Prince Charming waiting.
A roomful of friends,
A blackboard and numerous
scribblings and formulae,
Textbooks and notebooks
Covering "Mills and Boon's" story.
Some of us very serious,
Aspiring and high flyers,
Some even prefer
To stay calm as the sky
And smile like the sun.
Decades have passed since,

Friends are now miles apart.
Pages of memories write
The quarrels and prattlings
Of those frivolous times.
Aged eyes still yearn for
The roomful of friends
Laughing and waffling
Hand in hand, shoulder to shoulder,
Under the wise, old Jacaranda tree.

Equation

Always, I'm poor at Maths.
Never can I tally an equation,
Easy or tough.
Fistful of water seeps through
The chinks of scrawny fingers.
Cannot I count the rate of
The falling of water drops.
I just let them flow...

Sometimes I sit by my friend dear
She caresses my weary forehead
With her smooth, cool flowing fingers.
Inside her bosom she harbours
Orbs moving round and round...
She warbles and she giggles
I keep listening and counting her waves.
But I lose count, I fail—
Naturally.

The unvarying, unchanging,
Rigid, inert mountains
Cannot move me.
Rather, like a wizard, the
Ever-flowing tides
Bind me in a trance.

It was only the other day

That I was sitting by the rocks
And counting bountiful waves
And wondering,
'Since how long
We're in love, Davy Jones?'
As usually, I lost count.
Only then, I saw Calypso
Riding on a milky white wavy crest
And whispering, 'For eons, for eons, for eons!'

Conscious

As far as the canoe
Called Memory carries me
I can see a cavern on the top
Of a craggy mountain.
On the steep walls of the cave,
I see you sitting on your haunch
And the wall is being morphed
Into a colourful fresco.

The canoe veers into the
Bends of the Mediterranean sea,
I find you bending over a clay tablet,
Slowly the tablet gets morphed

Into the first heroic verse written by you—
"Gilgamesh!"

You named the pristine cavern
On the top of the ancient mountain-
"Alta Mira!"
Perspective that is lofty.
Come, once again let me
See you on the apex of Mt. Sinai,
With your sight travelling far and wide,
In search of a single humane mind!

Metamorphosis

I was awakened
The other day
By the tinkling drops of
Fresh morning dew upon
The leaves of the cherry tree
Which sheltered me.
A hairy me was startled to see
Myself lying in a dark tube,
The walls of which
Are wound in silk.

Cutting through the silky screen,
I came out with wobbling feet.

I got dazzled by the
Glare of yellow sunlight
With my dark, hairy trunk
I was about to crouch back
Into my dark, silky refuge,
Only then something fluttered
Upon my own body!
I couldn't believe my eyes—
Two pairs of silky dreams set onto my back!

Just as I was about to fly

My maiden flight,
The jealous eaves of Jacaranda
Whispered, “Such a glorious beauty!”

Little Boy

My little boy
Had a little toy.
Once he broke the toy
And it hurt my little boy.

My little boy
Fixed his toy

Brought that joy
To little boy.

My little boy
Used little loy,
Called out he, 'Hoy!'
In the farm soy.

My little boy
Had a round toy,
Called he that orb,
Trot he would globe,
In his long robe,
A pair of red gloves
To gather his treasure-trove.

Spectrum

The long shiny strands of
The tall palm tree
Oozes the molten gold
In its diurnal glory,

The white forest in
A wintry night bathes
In the silvery stream
Cascading from the heavens..

The pretty insect hops from
Buds to buds and takes pride
In its iridescent wings
That lends her grandeur

The imposing bird gracefully
Spreads its blue-green splendour
To show the world his beauty
Which he thinks abiding,

The eye of the heaven smiles
At all the earthly pride umpteen
Once the heaven closes the eye,
The earth loses all hues, all sheen.

Dream

A stack of golden hay
The morning merry and gay,
Little lad makes his way,
To his school not far away.

At school arrives he late,
The master stops him at the gate,
Asks, "What time is it, say?"
"Sir, harvesting caused my delay."

"You work in the field, not study?

"My father very sick, not sturdy,
I mind the field when he takes bed,
If I don't work, we won't have bread."

"Field labour or school hour—
Which is your choice?
Field with a goal-bar, sir,"
Spoke he in a low voice.

"Don't understand grammar, sir,
Or equations hard,
But I can make out the
Meanings of red or yellow card.

I dream to be a footballer, oh!
Like Messi or Ronaldo,
Everyday, I wish the paddy field to be
A good round football ground for me!"

Princess

I was combing my way
Through the pristine forest of Singalila,
Sturdy sticks in my hand,
To balance through the
Craggy sinewy path.

Array of varicoloured Rhododendron

Stood smiling on the way
To welcome us in
Their own generous way.
Here and there a buck with golden hide,
A red panda, a meek pangolin or
A yellow-throated marten peep in.

Crossing a wide, apple-green bugyal
I stepped into a fine woods of pine.
Faltering over a supine pine cone,
I was tempted to pick up one—
As I bent over, I heard clip-clop of hooves.
I looked up and saw
The most startling sight of the grove.
Cloaked in a sanguine robe of royalty,
Her lustrous ravine locks flowing freely
In the crispy air, she darted a smile at me

That caught me in her spell for eternity.

Treaty

On a crispy evening in early Spring,
We signed the treaty.
You and I,
To be partners in will and woe—
Vows written in black and white.

A number of feats and tasks

We handled together since,
At least tried to tackle schemes.
We made ventures—joint ones,
That took us to the icy hills,
To the frosty forests and cold uplands.
But not to the wild seas,
To the folds of warm waves.

On a wintry winter morning,
We signed a treaty.
You and I,
To become strangers
To each other heresoafter.
Together we never saw the wild waves,
Never felt the warmth of a blue Zephyr.

Chandraketugarh

In the deep of your bosom
You have ensconced a secret.
Many have tried hard,
To unearth the unknown.
Some succeeded, some failed,
Only a sliver came to be unveiled.
Annals, sagas, rumours float around,
That once you had wealth and grace abound.
Sailors, merchants from over the great seas
By your pastoral shore anchored their ships.

The astrologer Khana and astronomer
Varahamihira of yore,
Saw your sky, smelt your earth, O old
Chandraketugarh!

[Chandraketugarh is an ancient place in Bengal which was previously a prosperous port town and to which city the great astrologer Khana (between 9th and 12th century AD and the great astronomer Varahamihira (505-587 AD) belonged. There are many legends about them.]

Cloud-burst

On an early winter day
As the coy morning
Was blushing behind the
Fringes of fresh foliage
Of the hoary burflower tree,
And the birds were chirping merrily
With pretty coloured flies looking on
And collecting sugary nectar from blossoms
A thud was heard silencing all the other sounds.
A dinky monkey was sitting indifferently
On the top branches of a bokul tree.
It startled and looked.
All it could see...
Was the tall ancient mountain caved in,
Close-knit buildings on hills collapsing
Like house of cards only to be swept away
In the raging, spating waters of a fiery
Mandakini.

Familial

She went out of the office in time,
So that she could catch the train
That skips some stations to arrive
The destination minutes before time.
She boarded the train happily,
The train rolled on skipping stations
Making her joyous she could reach home early.

Suddenly the train halted, it stopped.
Time ticked off, the wheels did not move.
Impatience grabbed the confused passengers
And the platform bristled up with hurry and flurry
While it was announced that a blockade on
The rail tracks ahead had caused the delay
Which could be inordinate, even indefinite.

She grew anxious, she grew cautious and serious.
She had four children at home to look after,
She had no one else, on other relations—
She did not know now where her estranged husband was.
Her children meant the world to her,

What would become of them if she couldn't
reach home?
All the ominous thoughts thronged her mind
While the time ticked off,
And with a sudden jerk, the train moved.

She reached home, later than her usual time.
From the corner of the narrow lane she could
See her small, tiled roof house at the lane end.
Some others could also see her.
They were long waiting for her arrival.
Tense and worried, they came out of the house
To set their eyes fixed on the path.
Just as they spotted her, they rushed towards her
Barking, meowing, chattering and flattering in
joy—
Her children.

The Nymph

Once the princess of the Ocean
Fell in love with a king's son.
The prince had his palace
On shore, a grand, exotic place!
The princess was playing with waves,
The prince thought it to be
The mighty Ocean's grace.

The land and the water met,
The prince for a new life set.
"You're not an earthly man's daughter,
How can I hold your hand forever?
You're a sea fairy, a fish, a mermaid,
Not of our soil you're made."

The nymph had a crystal heart,
The prince's words left her deeply hurt.
The crystal was broken into pieces,
Far, far, afar swam away the princess.

It was the other day that you and I
Were gathering shells by the mighty bay.
I stumbled upon some shells unusual,
I bent, picked them and found them special.
The shells were crystals smithereens,

You took one and gasped watching their sheen—
"I know these pieces, but I don't know for how
long,"
Only then, far off from the sea
we could hear an exotic, lilting, ethereal song!

House

I want a house of mine
That would be made of bricks
Baked in the lights of love,
Cemented by dollops of care
And shaded with tiles of affection.
A stretch of terrace would
Encircle the entire house
That would face the east
To receive the first sheen of the sun,
And a courtyard to house trees
And plants and shrubs and creepers

That would receive all the green of Nature.
I would call it Home.

Light

A newborn opens its eyes
To this world strange.
From mother's womb
To the mother's lap
Is a moment of Revelation
For the new guest.
Then one day
The wobbling legs
Set out crawling to
Discover the world around
So that one fine morning
Two steady legs can walk
Up to the sandy shore to
Receive the bountiful first rays
With gratitude—
That once a warm lap with a warm smile
Held the tiny hands to show the lights of the
world.

Growing Up

As we grow up
We learn the
Ways of the world.
Wise people we
Think ourselves to be.
We jump up to give advices,
Although unsolicited sometimes.
The poor, the sick,
The meek and the helpless
Are favourite to us.
We like to pity them,
Our pity makes us look big.
Are we really big, big grown-up men?

Hunt

It drizzled all the way.
Walking through the
Tortuous paths all day,
The travellers were tired
And pitched tents
By the side of a cowshed
On the slope of the mount.
The weary eyelids soon closed,
Rapid rattles of the heavy drops
On the tents acted as a lullaby.
The night was shaken by a
Loud bellow and the walkers woke.
Parting the curtain of the tent
He tried to see what wronged the cattle.
His blood curdled to see two blazing
Eyes watching him by the side of his tent.

Fragile

Hold the glass tumbler tight,
As a moment's mistake might
Break the glass into pieces!
Take care of the pretty flower
As without care it will wither!
The fancy porcelain vase
May drop and break in case
It receives the slightest shiver!
Colourful balloons are fun to play
Give it a pop and it will burst away!
Blithesome bubbles come from a fizz,
A whiff of air and vanished it is!
Most fragile thing is on this earth
Trust—once broken, not to be repaired!

Snaps

The lovely place
With its pleasant grace
Enchanted us.
You kept clicking pictures,
Of the hills, the springs and flowers.
I did not take a snap,

Rather did I trap,
The vast pageantry of a fanciful world.

Camaraderie

In the journey called life,
We meet many faces.
Some are seasonal friends,
Some commit till the journey ends.
Many a hand offer to hold theirs,
Most of them fail to keep promises.
Only the true heart keeps
Holding till the world ends.

Walk

Crawling on all fours
And exploring the world
Is the first feat of a human child.
The steady legs then
All of a sudden
Stand on its feet
To claim his hold over the world.
Yet, a stumbling block on the path
Teaches the real walking!

Words

It takes one year two
To learn to speak how to.
Streams of words—old or new
Find an easy flow
From the tender mouth.

But it takes eons more,
Standing on the sandy shore
Of life to learn how to speak a word
That neither harms nor does hurt!

Saga

The tree stands tall
In the middle
Of the meadow.
In each season
The leaves fall,
New leaves green
Each season grows.
Tree trunk firm,
Not any storm
Shakes it though
Man's life so,
Keep changing stories—
Leaves, trunks and trees.

Thanksgiving

Keep meeting people,
Greet them with a smile
Because a good vibe
Always makes your life
On a jolly note thrive.
Be ever grateful
To those people
Who make you smile
Because without guile,
They are ones
Who like gardeners,
Tend the flowers
Of your soul
To bloom in full.

Asset

From day to night, you run,
You run to shine like the sun.
To see your hands glow
With steady sliver flow.
Your days are too busy counting silvers,
Ever seen the night sky and counted the stars?
Your mind is benighted with thoughts of
Opulence, wealth and assets lots of,
While through the gaps of your fingers
Slips out love—the asset most precious!

Beauty

All beauty lies in
The eyes that behold.
If the eyes are true,
If the intent is pure,
Beauty wins time,
And is truth for sure.

Sharing

It needs a spark
To light a candle.
As the candle burns,
The flame grows bigger
The candle grows smaller
Till it burns itself all.
But it never loses light
If, before the last drop,
The candle lights
Some more candles bright.

9 789360 940386

Printed by Libri Plureos GmbH in Hamburg, Germany